Digging for God

The best place to find God
is in a garden.
You can dig for him there.

—George Bernard Shaw.

Digging for God

Praying with Poetry

ANNE M. HIGGINS

ILLUSTRATIONS BY MAUREEN BEITMAN

RESOURCE *Publications* · Eugene, Oregon

DIGGING FOR GOD
Praying with Poetry

Resource Publications
An Imprint of Wipf and Stock Publishers
199 W. 8th Ave., Suite 3
Eugene, OR 97401
www.wipfandstock.com

ISBN 13: 978-1-60899-807-4

Manufactured in the U.S.A.

All scripture quotations are taken from the Holy Bible, New American version, NAB, copyright 1971, by Catholic Publishers, Inc.

Contents

Acknowledgments

"Tribute Poem" *How the Hand Behaves* Finishing Line Press 2009

"Second Antiphon in the Style of Hildegard" NCR February 21,2003

"Sister Anne Robb Writes a Letter" *How the Hand Behaves*; COMMONWEAL October 11,2002

"Go out to the Woods and Feel the Tree Bark" *How the Hand Behaves* Finishing Line Press 2009

"Sitz im Leben" SISTERS TODAY November 1983

"The Roofless Church" ANTIGONISH REVIEW Summer, 1982

"Rain on the Hedgerows" *At the Year's Elbow* Wipf& Stock Publications 2006

"Junk Drawer" *Scattered Showers in a Clear Sky* PlainView Press 2007

"The Snake Plant" WELLSPRING Winter 2001

"The Rose in the Chapel" NCR October 19, 2007

"Thomas Merton Checks on His Trees" WINDHOVER Spring, 2002

"Angry Enough to Die" LALITAIMBA

"Saying the Rosary" WINDHOVER Spring, 2002

"Garden Gloves Huddled" *How the Hand Behaves* Finishing Line Press 2009

"Heliotrope" SISTERS TODAY November 1981

"Perennials" *How the Hand Behaves* Finishing Line Press 2009

"Six" UMBRELLA Fall 2008

"At the Lake that was once a Volcano" THE MARS HILL REVIEW #20, 2002

Eden

Genesis 2:8–9

Tribute Poem

Praise for late sleeping day,
waking up without alarm,
for corkscrews,
corkscrew call of
yellowing lustful goldfinches,
butter,
opposable thumbs,
lusciously plush perfume
of viburnum
blooming in the woods
just now
just now.

Name five events, situations, or experiences that you appreciate—
go for the ordinary and undramatic ones.
Write a poem of praise to God for them.

Second Antiphon in the Style of Hildegard

O You who squeeze the wind
until she howls,
who wring the rain until
she gushes,
send electric waves
rushing through the cord
to jolt the vacuum cleaner
to roaring life,
I praise your power
moving in the homeliest of things.
Roses on couch cushions,
lamp stands, small city gardens,
bath water slipping down the drain,
steel wool scouring egg crust off the iron frying pan.

List five objects in your everyday life that you would call "the homeli-est things."

What gift does each of them have for you?

Sister Anne Robb Writes a Letter

Having turned in my stamps,
signed on to silence,
I dream
the old friends
open their empty mailboxes.
In dreams,
they come to visit,
dressed oddly,
staring and shy.
In dreams,
they shout out to me
from the other end of the church.

I trace their names
in the sand of my palm
and God
washes them
into Himself

Imagine yourself on the seashore, writing a letter to God in the sand. What do you say?

Summer Morning in the kitchen at Seton House

Sitting at the small square table
facing the window, refugee
from the country of longing
where clouds of grief
obscure the mountains,
country cooled by sorrow, heated by dread,
blasted by gusts of panic,
I finger the coffee cup.

Here, the weather is more benevolent.
Mild winds ruffle the oak tree.
The lavish sun ripens
hydrangeas and raspberries.

The intimate sound
of the hummingbird's
arrival at the feeder
interrupts my fragile silence.

Sit at your kitchen table at a quiet, solitary time. Pay attention to your surroundings— to what you eat and drink.

Imagine God sitting across the table from you.

What do you say to each other?

In Those Days

In those days,
the tree inhabited the living room,
dressy guest drinking water,
lulling me with balsam voice.
Long pine needles jabbed my lips
as I crouched beneath the spiny arms
basking in the tawdry magic
of twinkle lights.
Golden glass balls mirrored my five year old face.
Needles now pink, now yellow, now green on
my concave cheeks and brow,
brown hair tangled with tinsel.
In those days I would build
a small town under the tree,
cardboard houses with glitter glazed roofs
clutched the cotton snow,
a mirror turned into the frozen lake
the cricket sized skaters skirted,
the faithful ice full of the heaven
of tree branches.
In those days I stretched out
underneath the tree in the dark room,
to watch the lights make ever changing
color , ever changing dark patterns
on the wall above.

Remember a specific image from a Christmas from your childhood. Talk to God about what that image meant to you.

Wintering on St. Mary's Mountain

Lawnfrost, glittering sparrows,
lights in the twig taut trees.
In the cold sky,
planes, planets,
space stations.

Grey stone college buildings
on the paws of the mountain,
empty of students
gone for Christmas.

Icy wind shrugs off
mountain's hump.
Great mother bear of a mountain
emerges from hiding
when the leaves lawn her fur.
Rattlesnakes sleep in the
fat folds of her belly,
in the creases behind her knees.

Owls and woodpeckers
skim the gravestones—
buttons on her broad brown coat.

Recall your school life.

Picture your school buildings and surrounding natural scenery.

Imagine yourself walking those grounds with God.

What do you say to each other?

Nearsighted

Although the eye doctor's chart
 melted sadly into the wall ,
I can see this minute before me,
like a snowbird in the feeder
eighteen inches from my face.
We stare at each other through the window.
His black beady eye is watchful.

I also can see nouns and ruins,
 hairs on my arms,
  wrinkles on my hands,
  pulls in my stockings and pills in my sweaters.

I can see the ocean, near me in my mind.
that same bedroom window at Cape May
every summer for 14 summers,
can see it better than the snow squeezing the field.

I can see the hummingbird from five summers ago
better than I can see the finches this morning.
And I can see you, nearby,
on my clothes,
see you with warmth
that lingers.
My glasses
are adjectives,
they clarify,
they make my sight specific
even when they are smudged.

Do you wear glasses? If so, for how long?

What/Who can you see without them?

Talk to God about some things you know you need to see more clearly.

Ask God for the glasses of grace.

Springtime in Antioch

Acts 11:19–26

Silent green cells
glide through stem.
Leaves unfold
small green hands.
Sun calls
to applause.
We stir within
a city within,
turn slowly around ourselves,
a silent westerly movement.
like red blood cells
through arteries,
wings, corridors,
toward the heart.

Reflect on your community—Church community, Work community, wherever you feel most connected to others. Picture this group in organic images.

Speak to God about what you see.

Go Out to the Woods and Feel the Tree Bark

Dogwood, elephant grey, mostly smooth,
made small cracks.
Blue Spruce made deep ones, blueish gray,
hinting of moss.
The old Magnolia, intermittently smooth,
southern accent, waiting for those creamy blossoms,
genteel belle with speckled freckles, liver spots
on old lady hands.
Tulip Poplar, popular
for ropy twists, pretzel whorls
long veins curving around the trunk.
Young White Pine—smooth,
not much to say . . .
Chokecherry—grey sheen, rings of wrinkles,
horizontal scores.
Tree whose name I do not know,
wearing your cable knit sweater,
gnarled, snarling.

Take some time with the trees in your nearest grove , park, forest, or garden.

Feel the bark. What images come to you?

Sing a hymn of thanks to God for the trees.

Solomon

Songs 8:13

The Rose in the Chapel

The rose still blooms
in October's chilly breath.
After anticipated winters,
overlooked springs,
unnoticed summers,
it blooms.
Even after it is finally cut,
finally vased in
the home it grew for,
the rose blooms,
blossom parting its lips
in a morning song,
curving to the light.

Picture your favorite flower.

Use all your senses to experience it.

Offer it back to God.

Thank God for this delight.

Sitz im Leben

Who sits in my life
makes me rise like water
around him?
Who contains me
like wine in a bottle,
who dwells within
like light in a candle?
Athens backs away from him.
Corinth opens her arms.
His words make me
His arrow, hiding,
His hand, gloved.

Reflect on your situation in life.

What image do you have for yourself as an instrument of God?

Voice Mail

I have your voice from months ago
on the phone mail.
Electric voice tells me
my oldest message is thirty weeks old—
it's your voice there,
coming to me through the phone I cradle on my neck,
your voice saying my name.
It's a mundane message,
but it's your voice,
and I can't erase it.

A young man came to tell me
about his love for a girl back home.
"Isn't it silly," he said,
so embarrassed.
"I play her voice back
on the phone mail."

No, it is not silly.
Your voice triggers my longing.
I touch the sound of your voice
and a spasm of delight
and longing engulf me,
quickly followed by waves
of painful emptiness.
What message
does this voice mail have for me?

Do you have anyone's message saved on your voice mail?

Do you have anyone's voice saved in your auditory memory?

Picture that person, living or deceased. Hear that person saying your name.

Pray for that person.

The Pink Trees of Emmitsburg

It is the first of all mornings.
The curtain rises,
the mountains bow,
extend pointy fingers
to a huddle of pink trees,
tulle ballerinas
in a world of black tights.
The audience,
hitherto numb and slumped,
gasps.

The outlandish pink trees
shake their stiff crinolines
and the whole theater stirs.
The audience feels
loved like brides
in a world of divorces.

Too frilly,
too old-fashioned,
the critics huffed.
The management closed the show,
closed the whole theater.

Only the caretaker
sees the pink trees dance.
They still dance,
so out of hand,
so outlandishly beautiful,
to the wind's applause.

Recall the first tree you ever planted .

What kind was it?

Did it flower in the Spring?

How tall is it now?

Thank God for your ability to plant trees.

Elizabeth Seton: Light and Grace

Candlelight on her Bible.
She reaches for the pen, writes in the margin
"to know Thy truth."
To know, in the midst of
argument and controversy . . .
Candlelight flickers
as she underlines <u>Eternity.</u>
"Evenings alone: writing—Bible—
psalms in burning desires of heaven."

Sunlight pours through
the schoolroom window,
lighting her face,
the faces of the children.
It's the light of faith—
light to know.

Grace fills her words to the sisters,
her dear ones, clutching her hand
as they walk the summer valley,
grace in the presence
<u>"of you know who."</u>
Common sense lived out in love:
 spinning wheel in the kitchen,
 piano in the schoolroom,
folding open doors of the chapel—
grace to do.

Her words to a student far away:
"My heart has gone home with you."
Home with us, with
light to know,
grace to do.

Think of a teacher in your life who helped you value the things that really matter.

Thank God for that person.

The Roofless Church, New Harmony, Indiana

A poem on silence
sits on silence
like a leaf
on a still pool,
light, brittle,
brown as earth.

Silence, brown as earth,
we describe
by making walls around it
and describing
the walls.

In the center
of that roofless church,
a pear
whose seed is God.

Recall the silence you have experienced
as you have worked in your garden.
Recall God's presence there.

Sacre Coeur, Paris

In the Metro,
I could not feel the rain.
Emerging as from sleep
at the other end of Paris,
where the rain just stopped,
you were waiting,
waiting for me
on top of the highest hill.

Heart pounding speed
into my legs,
I climbed a million steps
to meet you.

Tired hitchhikers
sang beside your door.
Rain wet city
glistened at sunset,
stretched before your face.
You called stories out of our hands,
gifts out of our eyes.
You never closed for the night.

The stars rose down
on your round white crown
like halo,
like Bethlehem.

Think of a church building which has had an impact on you.

Picture it.

In your imagination, visit that building again with a friend who has never seen it.

Describe it to that friend as you walk through the church.

At the Seton High School Homecoming, 1975

Familiar paradox of presence:
a house well lived in.
Full house, moving like family
up the steps,
clusters of saddle shoes,
a minor silence
of talk and work:
high sunny rooms,
a freedom from bells.

Old books not gone
but shared.
Faces repeat
sister, mother,
grand-daughter.
Names repeat
old house, new family.

The chapel: presence—
stained glass windows
from fifty years
open. In comes God's wind
on the new stark walls
stained glass sunlight
on today,
familiar and new.

Saddle shoes
and modern haircut,
somebody's grandmother
tomorrow,
no one is nameless here
in this old house
of many talents, like the heart,
much more beautiful
when full.

Recall a school reunion, or a family reunion that you attended.

What, or who surprised you the most?

Talk to God about your discoveries, or about your desires for "reunion."

Rain on the Hedgerows

I do desire you, God.
Your touch like rain on my face,
rain on the landscape of my heart,
like a meadow full of weedy
brown late summer grass,
full of field sparrows,
tangled vines full of thorns and berries,
pokeberry, chokecherry, hackberry trees,
pull of cedar waxwings,
Your rain lingering like dew on that thicket
that is my heart,
that thicket of desires, thorns, thorny questions
and leaf-berry thick hidden places
where the warblers go to eat the purple berries
of my passions, my regrets, my dreams,
fears, imaginings,
a thick, overgrown path, Lord, wet with your rain,
growing and ripening all that fruit for your
Spirit to eat,
Your Spirit in the wings
Of a million birds passing through me.

Recall a time when you returned to a sacred place,
hoping to experience another manifestation of God.
What happened?

Garden Dweller

In the hibernation called January,
where frost crunches like sugar underfoot,
I feed the birds in the woodland garden
where jonquils and daylilies sleep.
Chickadees and titmice arrive at the first whistle,
their cousins close behind.
As I watch them eat,
I remember a young rabbit last June,
awkward, jumping for the sake of jumping,
regarding me as just another animal.
He uttered a birdlike chirp as he approached.
sniffed the gloves lying on the ground,
chewed the rubber around the cotton.
Coming closer,
 pulled on my shoestrings.
Then, standing like a statue, I felt his small paws
on my calves,
tentative,
investigating.
Satisfied , I suppose, that there was nothing there to eat,
he turned his attention to the clematis leaves.
In the cold sleeping afternoon,
I survey this kingdom of dead leaves and mud,
vigilant.

Recall a time when you were surprised by the behavior of some wild creature.

Thank God for that gift of Nature's touch.

Gethsemane

John 18:1–2

Vineyard Stories

One son was invited and he said yes
and he did not come.
The other one said no
and regretted it
and came.
Was that the same son
who was killed by all those
tenant farmers?
Were those farmers
the ones
who worked all day
and got the same pay
as the ones who came
at the last horn's blow?
Did all this happen
in the same vineyard
that glistens in the evening sun
where the lovely macramé of
green strings
reaches out
for the anchoring pole?
Grapes are heavy in the
September air.
Here is a place for
the liar and the rash.
Here is time to say no
and change your mind.
Here, also,
the jealous
and the killer.
Here, harvest.

Remember a time when you said "No" and then changed your mind.

Remember a time when you said "Yes" and did not follow through on your commitment.

Talk to God in more depth about one of them.

Junk Drawer

I've always had one.
Before, it contained
Mittleschmertz:
Loose wire
Coffee stained spoons
Wrinkled Kleenex
Paper clips
Loose change
Business cards
Stamps
Tops of ballpoints
Dried up erasers

Now,
Weltshmertz:
Lower comfort
Mushy cardboard
Wrinkled calendar
Lacy raisins
Waterspilled paper
Crusted nails
Duty sunflower seeds
Old batteries.

Where is your junk drawer? In the kitchen? In your desk? In your bedroom?

What's in your junk drawer?

If there was a junk drawer in your heart, what would you find there?

Talk to God about an object you've found, and its significance in your life.

My Pattern is my Prison

A long numb drought—
the loneliness that drove me to this place—
the pensive kitchen—
so I believe in yesterday.
I'm cornered by my circumstance—
The tenuous quality of listening—
the lens is critical—
to disenthrall my self
I stretch my arm in hemlock, lilac, pine.
I feel bereft of must, bereft of summer.
The raspberry's a seasonal and fragile fruit.
I'm not yet free to lose my reputation.

What is the pattern that imprisons you?

What reputation are you afraid to lose?

Talk to God about your chains.

The Snake Plant

Roots so strong
that they break the clay pot
they live in.

Are sins my skin
which stretches as I grow,
and splits and falls away,
so that the roots are free?
Are my sins the bonds
which keep me small,
or hold me together?

The House of Change is red clay,
bigger inside than out.
Scouring the mineral deposits,
cleaning the crusty dirt
took the skin off my hands.

Recall a time when you moved a pot-bound plant to a new home.

Do you remember the violence of the re-potting?

Talk to God about when you experienced re-potting.

The Rich Young Man

As I walked away from him,
I thought of hell
in Springtime.
I said to the disciple at the doorway,
"Excuse me-
I really must go."
I walked the curving green where the sign said OUT,
back to the bustling town,
back to the home suddenly substitute,
my own words ring in my coward ears.

I still love this joyous life I have;
I store the happiness of each day,
giving it away as fast as I gain it.
But now is the first Spring after,
and in this green day my winter-bare answers crumble.
I clutch the lonely jewel-days to my yearning heart,
and come late to everything.

How are you like the Rich Young Man?

Talk to God about the ways you've run away from His call.

Gift Giving Time

For my friend,
taste of raspberry sherbet
melting into a glass of apricot nectar,
smell of lilacs,
sound of wood thrushes
calling to each other in the dew,
feel of sleek warm fur
on the ear of the retriever,
sight of yellow irises
in slanting evening light.

For my enemy-
taste of soap on the tongue,
the smell of crabmeat gone bad,
earsplitting wail of fire alarm,
feel of slimy rotten tomato,
the sight of dying frog,
on its back,
frog arms flailing weakly,
already gutted by crows.

Imagine a gift you would like to give to your friend.

Then, imagine a gift you would like to give to your enemy.

Talk to God about your feelings about these gifts, and pray for the recipients.

Thomas Merton Checks on His trees.

I sit on the bed above the chimneys.
Palmetto trees,
willows, live oaks,
disappear into the candlelight
blue in the solstice light,
air still warm,
red camellias blooming in the garden below.

I sit on the bed,
thinking sunset
over the mountain in Maryland,
 deer leaping in the empty battlefield,
grey deer with tree bark
in snow scattered grey grass.

I sit on the bed,
thinking Thomas Merton
walking Kentucky woods
in blue December light
twenty years ago,
checking on trees he planted
in anguish,
 loblolly pines grown tall and graceful,
bending in the sharp December wind,
taller still
twenty years later,
 trees he planted in anguish.

I sit on the bed,
checking on trees I planted:
Pink crab apple trees twenty years ago,
palmettos tonight.

What trees have you planted in anguish?

Picture them.   How tall are they now?

The Presence of Crows, Halifax

I've been longing to see the flash of black,
gold, white, the evening,
the evening grosbeak,
but all I see,
all that greets me from the lawn
are crows— murders of them.
One befriended by the lure of peanuts,
less wary, less skittish,
but bright black eye shining
in shining black head
eyes me
black feet walk toward me
toward the peanut at my feet.
How near will he come?
He has a call I've not heard before
from any bird.
Is he calling for company to share the peanut?
It's a rolling of sound out of his back,
a wave of sound like a human sound,
invitation, a comment of welcome.
In this northern country
I long to see the birds
who never come our way,
but all I get is
an abundance of crows.

What have you been longing to see?

What have you been seeing instead?

What could God be telling you in this discrepancy?

Angry Enough to Die

God found Jonah and asked him, "Have you reason to be angry?"
"I have reason to be angry," Jonah answered God,
"Angry enough to die."

My shady gourd plant is gone,
my cucumber, my castor,
under which I sheltered,
within which I hid.
Now I grope for the sky, that false mirror,
hot, burning my skin,
skin cancer blossoming like a dandelion.
I have reason to be angry.

I have still not tasted
the flavor of my tears,
where the sand yellow leaf blossoms a watchful hawk,
though the leaf borer makes lace of his breast
so the grey sea gapes through it.
Angry enough to die.

I'll eat and drink till my heart chars,
til that sunset burns clear through.

He is not speaking,
I lower my concrete mask
and listen.

Recall a time when you were angry with God.
What did you do? What did you say to God?
Did you hear God say anything back?

Golgotha

John 19:41, 20:15

Digging for God

I want to put my arm into the tunnel
provided by the groundhogs,
and keep digging
until I find God
so I can ask Him,
How come the weeds are still green
when the grass is brown with drought?
How come the only thing flourishing
now in the dried up, hard pan , heat baked soil
of the garden in the woods
is the Poison Ivy?

What do you want to ask God?

How do you dig for God? Where do you dig for God?

Japanese Beetles

In this light, my spirit was through all things and into all creatures,
and I recognized God in grass and plants.

-JACOB BOEHME

Varieties of green on the trees outside the window:
on the sun-side, iridescent, lime green
on the shade side, dark green.
at the top, just a few leaves responding to the
attentions of the light wind
with a coy tilt of their hands.

Look out three dimensions into
a tunnel of trees,
 a grassy floor,
mottled lime and lizard green
in the sun's fickle focus.

Japanese Beetles charge.
Sex crazed from the pungent scent,
they crash into me , away from the dahlias,
on their way to the lure
and sure death by suffocation.

Crusted on a peach pink peace rose,
like two dozen shiny green-brown jewels,
vampires of the summer,
cannibals of the flower flesh.

Into the bag they go,
unable or unwilling to fly back out,
fester among themselves
like a stampeding crowd
in the fire filled nightclub.

I see God in the trees, in the vulnerable roses.
I see God in the Japanese Beetles
whom I lure and trap,
but who keep coming at me
in unwelcome droves.

∿ ∿ ∿

What pesters you and threatens your garden?

Mother Seton's Bible

Mercy was your favorite word.
How many times
underlined in psalm and margin
by your wondering hand.
Mercy -on your eye
tears,
the sea, and thanks.
Mercy— vows
in an underground chapel-
let us not forget
our communion
of tomorrow.
Mercy-
thinking sea voyages,
passages to heaven,
thinking
how children breathe
their first
earth.

Flip through the pages of your Bible. Notice the passages you've marked. What seems to be your favorite word?

Talk to God about that word— what you have heard from Him through it.

Saying the Rosary

I used to say it on St. Paul Street
in bed, to go to sleep,
that small brown rosary
from the souvenir store at the catacombs in Rome…
Cecilia lying on her side, her hair swept back, the slice in her neck.
How I used to fall asleep saying it, lying on that sofa bed in the
octagonal living room,
in my light night gown,
with the traffic pouring by outside,
and the window fan on,
in the heat of the summer night,
praying to be spared from robbers
and rapists,
praying for sleep
to pull me quickly and safely to the morning.
and he filled me with a song I never sang,
A rose I never saw,
waves too distant for birds.

Do you say the Rosary? If so, where is your favorite place to say it?

Talk to God about how you feel when you say the Rosary.

Say the Rosary, picturing the people who are mysteries to you.

Say the Rosary, picturing the people you need to forgive.

Vincent de Paul

Wine and hundredfold
my father's name,
eating old food,
walking,
the man sleeping in the corner
by your house
smells like death,
but you wake him.
The streets reek,
the crowds press,
all the passages are interdict,
but you walk through them.
Your hands are grimy,
You have slept in your clothes,
You have never tasted ice.
Wine and hundredfold,
my father's name.

What is your father's name? Do you know its origins? Its meaning?
How do you feel when you say your father's name?

If Memory Serves Me

If Memory serves me,
she's falling down on the job.
Very slow to retrieve,
from the crevices in the upholstery,
the names of students I taught last year.
Sloppy about dusting off
my awareness of things to be done.
She skips the sticky places of regret on the floor,
the wallet left behind in the ladies room.
She makes me travel the stairs twice,
and deserts me when I reach the top.
Not until the gnats cloud my face in the garden
does she show me the bug spray
still back in my closet.
She's getting less reliable each year.
Slow-moving and ponderous,
she shuffles along the corridor,
thick-legged, swaying into the wall.

Personify your memory. Give him/her a name.

What does he/she look like?

What would you like him/her to retrieve for you?

My Father, at 92

At two o'clock today he declared
"Well, it's time to go."
"Where?" I asked
"Where?" my blind and deaf mother asked.
"Home."
"But you are home." we said.
"You've been living here eight years," I said.
"since you were eighty-four."

My father, now unsteady on your feet,
you don't remember your location, your wallet, your keys,
but you do remember
when I ran out in front of
oncoming traffic one day,
after kindergarten.
You were on the other side of the street.
You said it was because I was
already nearsighted
and no one knew it yet.
I recall
it was because
I didn't notice the oncoming traffic—
All I saw was you,
YOU, I saw clearly,
and still do,
standing on the other side of the street,
waiting for me.

Who stands on the other side of the street, waiting for you?

Speak to God about them.

Speak to them.

Garden Gloves Huddled

in a paper bag hanging on a hook
by the window where the ice clotted
bare branches quiver
and the sun sends their gnarled shadows on the snow below.

Garden gloves clean , soft, bleachy perfume,
stained brown and green,
some holy fingers clutch each other
While they wait.

Reflect: What are you waiting for this winter?

Heliotrope

Rare purple flower,
blue-eyed miracle,
you have bloomed for me.

I have seen you
wind your blind face to the sun,
stretch your thin leaf
in the darkest corner
to the suns voice calling poetry -
a word that your near deafness
hears.

Like heliotrope,
the eyes of that senile poet
in the nursing home.
I walked up to her bed like Jesus
and called poetry
poetry
do you live with it?

Like winter light
slipping round the corner
into a forgotten room,
like heliotrope to the sun,
her face turned lucid
floodlights
from her shriveled mouth
called poetry
poetry!
In a great bottomless
woman's voice.

Then, like the sun
sliding behind the hills

on that brief afternoon,
so her eyes
gradually dimmed again
into poems of sleep.

~ ~ ~

Think of a flower from your garden.

What human qualities do you associate with it?

What friend or loved one does it remind you of?

Hymn to Longwood Gardens

How is it that I was born five miles from you,
born to walk your three hundred acres for twelve years?

Now, thirty years later,
in the satiny iced lawns of February,
I dream of your sumptuous beds
of lavender
glowing numinous in summer twilight,
your solitary fountain
stumbled upon in deep shade,
of thrush revealing her speckled breast in the mulch
behind the Italian water gardens.

I dream of my first love
plucking my hand into his,
a young, thin, fine, freckled hand,
the first holding of hands
as we entered the garden
for a fountain display
on a starlit July evening.

In those days, you were free.
Now, you have flourished,
and your entrance fee is costly.

Reflect: In your life, what used to be free, and now is costly?

Wait for the Lord with Courage

Cardinals can sing long conversations
in serenity.
Perched on telephone wires at noon,
in the mountains, red throats
undulate with music.
Wait in the grey dawn, shivering,
for the short rip of punctuation
that announces
Pentecost.

Recall a celebration of Pentecost in your life.

How did it energize you?

How did it give you courage?

Revelation

Revelation 22:1–2

Five Stones

Belief is the engine that makes perception happen.
—FLANNERY O'CONNOR

Five stones on my windowsill.
Not smooth, not from the wadi,
burned by the river,
sucked by the beach,
pocked by the waterfall,
jagged by lightening,
creamed by time.

The word of God came to me thus,
in the sunlight sparking from their edges:
love,
use,
weeping,
rage,
food.
Somebody's down on the shore
cooking breakfast.

Write down five of your favorite words.

Imagine you join the Risen Jesus down by the seashore, as He cooks breakfast for you.

Share your five words with Him.

Towards March

Trees shake their shoulders restlessly.
What to do with those wandering
songs we used to sing?
Singing about Autumn in a Summer Song...
What is the season for leaving
when is there no more leaving?

Wines age gracefully, though
some sour
when opened.
You should drink some of them
six hours after they are bottled.

Old loves
here at the creek ,
wild phlox blooming still.

What flowers do you associate with your childhood? With your first
   love?

Watching the Plants Come Up

In March,
the slow concentrated watching begins.
In earliest morning light,
hesitating to start the trip to work,
the gardener stalks the rock garden,
notes breakthrough of daffodils
two inches up, tentative green,
pushing out from under
the last crumbled autumn leaves.

The gardener then monitors
embryonic leaves
of chrysanthemums,
green rosettes of sedum,
butter knife blades of iris
clustering around
last summer's
brittle, bent stalks.

More quickly than the crocus,
the bean seeds rise
in June.
The gardener awaits the remembered
first strong green arms
elbowing their way out ,
clots of earth still clinging.

It is hard to open the car door,
to climb into its cold
gassy arms
and go off to work
when each morning
a revelation waits
at home.

Recall your experience of watching the plants emerge in your garden.

Which ones do you see?

Remember your feeling as you saw them.

Talk to God about revelations in your life.

Perennials

Lambs ears flourish, creased gray, furry,
new growth out of rain's far fury.
Sneezewort carries cups of pearl;
white buds open on grace green stems.
Hosta— plates, pipes, ridges, rims,
Coneflower gems of purple whorled.

Sedum rosettes beyond counting,
roots fat carrots, land lust mounting,
seek earth's fountain, wide beneath.
Gardeners rest with these guests planted,
take low maintenance for granted,
fingers caress cream cusp of leaf.

What comes up easily for you, year after year— in your garden, and in your heart?

August Red

Salvia red salvation,
scarlet sage blossoms bend
in the roasting window box.
Regal red cardinal flowers
process down rows in the rock garden.
Flame red cannas lilies languish,
high as the crimson August sun
searing the blood thick air
where the ruby throat oars in,
tongue full of fiery nectar.

What blooms in your garden in high summer?

At the end of Wasbee Range

Charleston: old, hot,
tropically aristocratic,
short , crowded , closed in on itself.
Clotted white plaster walls,
crumbling brick walls,
peeling paint on wood walls of even the newer houses,
the ones built after the
War of Northern Aggression.

But Wasbee Range ,
the alley behind our house,
could be the castle grounds in Sleeping Beauty.
Overgrown with weeds,
coiling with briars from the resentful witch,
Wasbee Range abounds with bricks waterlogged too many
times,
rats in the rotten wood of the Dependency.

At the end of Wasbee Range,
in an untidy garden,
palmetto bugs scurry around the cracked cement.
In castle grounds left to themselves,
mulched with pine needles, gummy and
grey with mildew,
Ajuga struggle to spread,
camellias deliver their stunted pink blooms,
 sweet olive spits a small fragrance.
Everything needs pruning.

In the cul de sac of Wasbee Range , a garden of
the neighbor's musty garage,
everyone's trash cans,
the bottom end of
everyone's back yard.

Picture the bottom end of your backyard.

What lies there, overgrown and weedy, riddled with bugs?

Talk to God about what you would like to do there.

On the Ladder in the Laundry

Fabric fans
ruffled, crisp as taffeta,
husky stalks,
finger thick,
sturdy jungle green,
carrot smell
jumps to my touch,
flings into the air,
shouts when I break
off a leaf.

No flowers yet.
Lavish display of
leaf and stem
spark a litany to
all the geraniums
ungainly crowded
in a sunny window
of my memory...

Geranium on the ladder in the laundry,
pruned by those who wait for their clothes,
Geranium on the bookcase in the classroom,
flexing your arms in the carbon dioxide,
Geranium weedy, rescued from frost,
Geranium resplendent in the courtyard,
white blossoms glowing
in the chalky moonlight.

What grows in the sunny window of your memory?

Visualize it.

Talk to God about it.

Six

Sides to my story:
hidden fruits of the Holy Spirit,
sweet and delicious as raspberries.
Half of the Apostles—Half of the Tribes-
which ones?
Desks in the rows of my fifth grade classroom,
bedrooms in the house in Windsor Hills
whose trees I loved.
Lily bulbs now in the earth,
silently stretching their ghostly roots.
Peanut butter crackers in the pack I
gave my father,
who no longer has eyes for them.
Cans of Rolling Rock in their dangerous
plastic bracelets,
Pence,
no longer in use,
but pensive all the same.

How many sides are there to your story?

Describe them.

At the Lake that was once a Volcano

Deep green firs
spike dark and close.
We walk the soft slope.
As it crests,
a forty foot sky blue circle
rises to us,
bluer than twilight on a snowfield,
blue clear down to its two mile floor,
deepening as it falls.

Brush rustles out
grey bird rare as righteousness,
begging, boisterous,
feeds her young within our reach.

Golden Eagle,
enormous as hunger,
fans out through the blue air.

Fifty foot snow drifts
thaw to gritty grey
at the rim of the cliff,
two mile deep silence
draws us
to the bowl of thirst.

Recall a distant place to which you have travelled, a place that silenced you with its beauty.

Thank God for that place.

On Clearing Sr. Jean Marie's Garden

I knew they were out there.
Thirty years ago, I watched her work them.
Old then, with a hump on her back,
in full habit and veil, she hauled gallons of water
to keep them alive.

Thirty years later, I'm back.
Her name is on a grave in the cemetery nearby.
I took my rake and started the search.

First I found the stones large as bread loaves
which she placed around each house-sized space.
Under decades of leaves,
the daffodils waited, blankets of hyacinths,
duvets of lilies of the valley.

By July I had found the twelve stars,
cement, five-pointed, each large as my outstretched hand,
arranged in the ground in a room-sized oval.
Within, egg sized stones embedded, described a cross
 entwined with the letter M.
She had made the design of the back of her Medal,
enclosed it with a fine brick border.
In which heat soaked summer had she made this prayer?

Now Spring, her garden blooms profusely,
filling the woods with its fragrance.
Virginia bluebells flourish
inside the Miraculous Medal.

Reflect on a time when you were searching for a hidden, long—neglected object from your family history.
Did you find it?
Talk to God about your discoveries.

Gardener's Magnificat

My heart shudders in God's loamy breath,
and I stand silent before my flourishing garden,
for God has called his love for me
through the song of the Wood Thrush,
through sunlight and shadow on Iris and Peony.
God shines in the leathery purple Ajuga leaves,
startles me with feathery Astilbe
I thought long lost to me.

God's mercy rains on proliferating Thyme.
God's humor confounds my illusions of control
with unexpected volunteer Coleus,
with galloping Crabgrass.

God favors me with strong hands,
graces me with color and fragrance.
I praise Him with my toil,
with the gift of my bendable back.

God upholds His promise of fruitfulness
lived through Jesus,
present in my garden,
and in my heart.

Write your own gardener's Magnificat. What plants will you include? What are your surprises? Your losses? Your gifts?

www.ingramcontent.com/pod-product-compliance
Lightning Source LLC
Chambersburg PA
CBHW070502090426
42735CB00012B/2657